Drawing Legendary Monsters
Drawing Unicorns
AND OTHER MYTHICAL BEASTS

Steve Beaumont

New York

Published in 2011 by The Rosen Publishing Group, Inc.
29 East 21st Street, New York, NY 10010

Artwork and text: Steve Beaumont and Dynamo Limited
Editors: Kate Overy and Joe Harris
U.S. Editor: Kara Murray
Designer: Steve Flight

Library of Congress Cataloging-in-Publication Data

Beaumont, Steve.
 Drawing unicorns and other mythical beasts / by Steve Beaumont.
     p. cm. — (Drawing legendary monsters)
 Includes index.
  ISBN 978-1-4488-3251-4 (library binding) — ISBN 978-1-4488-3261-3 (pbk.) — ISBN 978-1-4488-3262-0 (6-pack)
 1. Art and mythology—Juvenile literature. 2. Animals, Mythical, in art—Juvenile literature. 3. Drawing–Technique—Juvenile literature. I. Title.
 NC825.M9B43 2011
 743'.87—dc22

                                            2010023600

Printed in China
SL001630US

CPSIA Compliance Information: Batch #WA11PK: For Further Information contact Rosen Publishing, New York, New York at 1-800-237-9932

CONTENTS

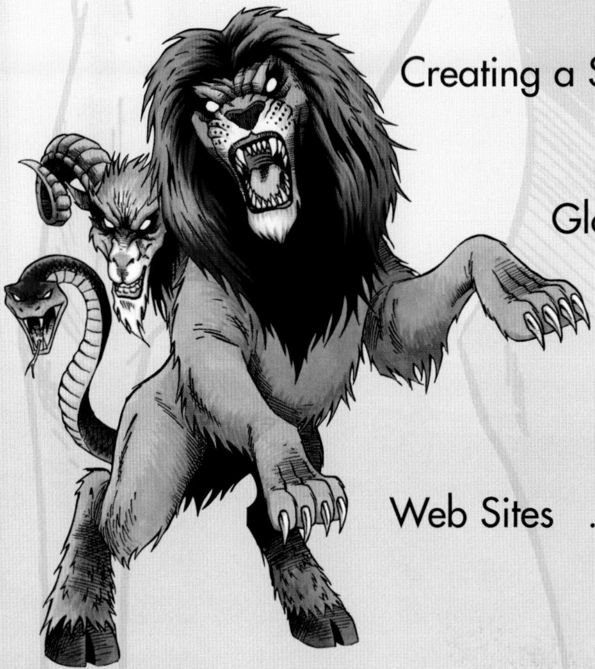

GETTING STARTED

Before you can start creating fantastic artwork, you need some basic supplies. Take a look at this guide to help you get started.

PAPER

Layout Paper

It's a good idea to buy inexpensive plain paper from a stationery shop for all of your practice work. Most professional illustrators use cheaper paper for basic layouts and practice sketches, before producing their final artworks on more costly paper.

Heavy Drawing Paper

Heavy-duty, high-quality drawing paper is ideal for your final drawings. You don't have to buy the most expensive brand – most art or craft shops will stock their own brand or a student brand. Unless you're thinking of turning professional, these will do just fine.

Watercolor Paper

This paper is made from 100 percent cotton, so it is much higher quality than wood-based paper. Most art shops stock a large range of weights and sizes. Using 140-pound (300 gsm) paper will be fine.

PENCILS

Buy a variety of graphite (lead) pencils ranging from soft (#1) to hard (#4). Hard pencils last longer and leave less lead on the paper. Soft pencils leave more lead and wear down quickly. #2 pencils are a good medium option to start with. Spend time drawing with each pencil and get used to its qualities.

Another product to try is the mechanical pencil, in which you click the lead down the barrel using the button at the top. Try 0.5mm lead thickness to start with. These pencils are good for fine detail work.

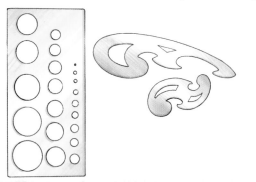

CIRCLE TEMPLATE

This is useful for drawing small circles.

FRENCH CURVES

These are available in several shapes and sizes and are useful for drawing curves.

INKING AND COLORING

Once you have finished your pencil drawing, you need to add ink and color. Here are some tools you can use to get different results.

PENS

There are plenty of high-quality pens on the market these days that will do a decent job of inking. It's important to experiment with a range of different ones to decide with which ones you are comfortable working.

You may find you end up using a combination of pens to produce your finished artworks. Remember to use a pen with waterproof ink if you want to color your illustrations with a watercolor or ink wash. It's usually a good idea to use waterproof ink anyway as there's nothing worse than having your nicely inked drawing ruined by an accidental drop of water!

PANTONE MARKERS

These are versatile, double-ended pens that give solid, bright colors. You can use them as you would regular marker pens or with a brush and a little water like a watercolor pen.

BRUSHES

Some artists like to use a fine brush for inking linework. This takes a bit more practice and patience to master, but the results can be very satisfying. If you want to try your hand at brushwork, you should invest in some high-quality sable brushes.

WATERCOLORS AND GOUACHE

Most art stores stock a wide range of these products, from professional to student quality.

CERBERUS

According to ancient Greek mythology, the fearsome three-headed dog Cerberus is not only a monster, but also the guard of the gates to the underworld. The souls of the dead can never return to the land of the living under his powerful gaze.

1

Draw the stick figure. Cerberus has three heads, so include three circles. He has four legs and paws, like a dog. Don't forget a curved line for the tail.

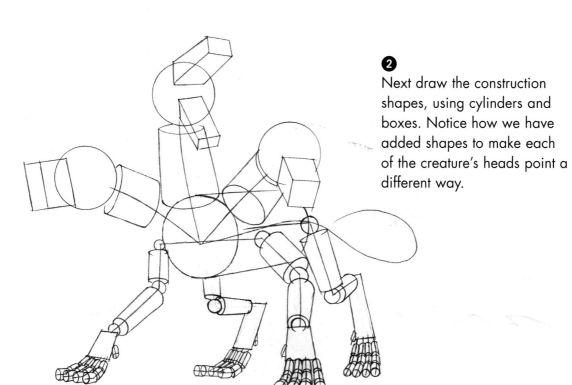

2
Next draw the construction shapes, using cylinders and boxes. Notice how we have added shapes to make each of the creature's heads point a different way.

3
Now draw the three heads. Focus on the snarling mouth, with its open jaws and sharp teeth as well as the eyes and nose. Add the skin outline and develop the paws and claws.

4

Erase your construction shapes. Then give Cerberus the chains around his necks. Add lines to emphasize the contours of his body.

5

Now clean up the drawing. Add shading and more detail to the body and chains. Draw saliva dripping out of the beast's jaws to make him look ferocious.

TOP TIP

Inking the contours on the creature's body and its neck tendons will emphasize its strength and give the impression it is barking.

6
Carefully ink over the finished pencil drawing.

7

Add color to your drawing to make the animal look even more angry and frightening.

Use a medium gray for the base followed by layers of darker, warmer grays.

Apply cool gray for the chains. Create a rust effect by using sandy yellow and orange with a hint of green.

UNICORN

The beautiful and peace-loving unicorn takes its name from the Latin for "one horn." The curling horn in the centre of its forehead acts as an antidote to any poison. Magical and untameable, it can only be captured by an innocent young girl.

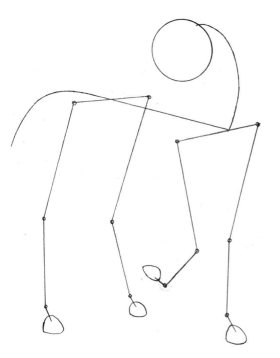

1
Start with the horse-like stick figure. Draw an angled line curved at the end for the back and tail and four stick legs with hooves. You also need a curved line for the neck.

2

Add the construction shapes, using one large wide cylinder for the body and long, thin cylinders for the legs. Notice how the neck is a series of balls.

Take a look at pages 6–7 for more tips on how to draw horses.

3

Next shape the unicorn's head and add detail to the face. Draw the pointed horn, making sure the outer lines are straight. Add the skin.

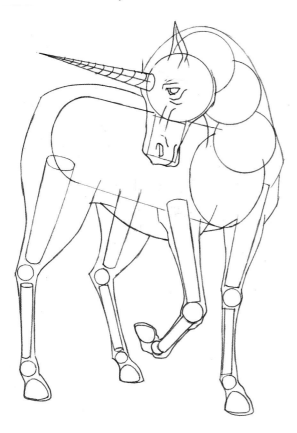

4

Erase your construction shapes, then add the wild mane and tail. Draw contour lines to show the strength of the neck.

TOP TIP

Stick to simple shapes when drawing hair. We've used a reversed S shape for the mane and the tail is a C shape on its side. Notice how the curves give a sense of movement.

5

Heavily shade the underbelly of the unicorn and the top of its tail. Lightly shade the contour lines to bring out the muscles. Fill in the eye and nostril.

6

Ink over the pencil drawing.
Work carefully on the eye,
leaving white highlights.

7

This drawing has been colored using a pale gray base followed by a layer of pale blue.

Create the dappled skin with a blender marker. This type of pen has a colorless ink in it, which spreads the colors underneath when you pull it across the page.

TOP TIP
You can also create dappling with a paintbrush when using watercolors. Load the brush up with a small amount of water and gently dab the colored areas you want to blend.

Apply pale violet to the underbelly, inner leg, and top of the tail to create a darker tone. Then add dark blue and dark gray.

CHIMERA

The Chimera is a grotesque and terrifying creature from Greek mythology. A hybrid with the heads of a lion, goat, and serpent, it devastated human populations until its death at the hands of Bellerophon, a hero and slayer of monsters who rode on the winged horse, Pegasus.

1 Start with the skeleton stick figure. Include two circles and a triangle for the lion's, goat's, and snake's heads that form part of this four-legged beast.

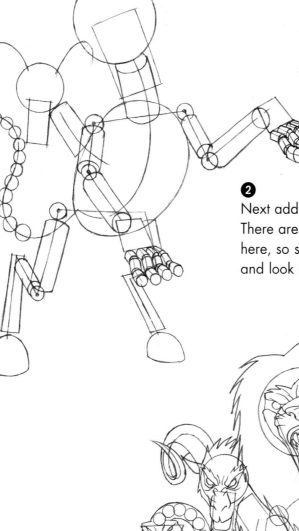

2

Next add the construction shapes.
There are lots of different shapes
here, so spend time on this stage
and look closely at the drawing.

3

Now draw the heads and develop
the faces. Notice how each one is
fierce, with narrowed eyes.
Outline the lion's mane and turn
the back feet into cloven hooves.
Draw around the construction
shapes to add form to the picture.

4

Remove the construction shapes. Then work on the shaggy fur around the body and add more detail to the mane and faces. Give the beast its sharp front claws.

Use cross-hatching for shading the snake's scales. This technique involves drawing overlapping diagonal lines in two different directions.

5 Give the Chimera a stronger form by adding shading. Work heavily on the lion's mane and keep your pencil sharp for all the fine detail elsewhere.

6

Ink over the final pencil drawing. Make sure the area around the lion's mouth is a dark solid block so that the fierce jaws stand out.

7

By coloring your work, you can add even more drama.

Use a sand-colored base for the goat's head. Then go over this with gray tones.

Use dusky red, orange, and brown for the lion's mane and snake's scales.

Apply white mixed with pale yellow for the snake's belly.

Start with a beige base for the main body. Build up strength of color with sandy yellow and pale orange.

Use midrange gray for shading on the fur.

CREATING A SCENE: THE FOREST GLADE

Medieval legends tell us that unicorns live in the most remote parts of forests and generally avoid human contact. So you would have to be very lucky indeed to catch a glimpse of one! But here's an opportunity for you to draw one in its natural habitat.

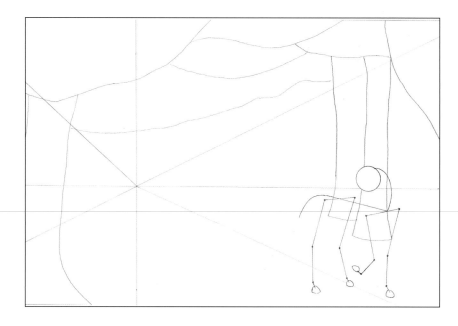

1 The key to drawing a convincing forest scene is depth. Remember your vanishing point and begin to build general layers, which can be filled in later with plants and trees, paying particular attention to the treetops to help build the appearance of a hidden glade.

2 Add in the trunks of the trees in your forest. Think about the angles and thicknesses of the trunks and remember that all trees grow differently. By varying the thicknesses and angles, you will help to create a more organic look.

3 It's time to add the leaves at the tops of your trees. Decide what sort of a look you would like. Plenty of leaves and coverage will give a quiet tone to your forest, whereas sparse growth will add a more sinister depth to the image.

4 Build your shading gradually, bearing in mind that the leaves will stop a lot of your light source from above from showing through fully. Remember that variety in shapes and textures is the key to making a more believable forest scene.

5 Keep your shading light, using it to add texture to the trees and rocks. If you are too heavy with the shading, you are in danger of creating a darker and more forbidding place, rather than the ethereal glade where you might meet a unicorn.

6 As the majority of the colors you will be using here will be greens, this image is a real exercise in building up the depth of color, getting darker as you head backward. It's best to start by coloring the higher leaves and working your way down.

GLOSSARY

complex (kom-PLEKS) Made up of many connected parts.

cross-hatching (KRAWS-hach-ing) A shading technique in which crisscrossing diagonal lines are overlapped to make an area of shadow.

cylinder (SIH-lin-der) A shape with circular ends and straight sides.

develop (dih-VEH-lup) To further or continue something.

ethereal (ih-THIR-ee-ul) Rare and magical.

focus (FOH-kis) To concentrate.

glade (GLAYD) An open space without trees in the middle of a forest.

habitat (HA-buh-tat) The place where an animal or plant is usually found.

tendon (TEN-dun) A tissue that connects bones and muscles.

vanishing point (VAN-ish-ing POYNT) The point at which the lines showing perspective in a drawing meet each other.

INDEX

WEB SITES

Due to the changing nature of internet links, PowerKids Press has developed an online list of Web sites related to the subject of this book. This site is updated regularly. Please use this link to access the list:
www.powerkidslinks.com/dlm/unicorn/